ESSENTIAL
STORAGE

TERENCE
CONRAN
ESSENTIAL
STORAGE

THE BACK TO BASICS GUIDE TO HOME DESIGN, DECORATION & FURNISHING

conran
OCTOPUS

Contents

14

Planning & Assessment

INTRODUCTION

PLANNING &
ASSESSMENT
TYPES OF
STORAGE
AREA BY AREA

Castagnaccio
• Salt
• Chestnut Flour
• Olive Oil
• Rosemary
• Raisins
• Walnuts
• x 20 mins
180°C

Introduction

Homes house things as much as the people that live in them. How and where we keep our belongings has a huge impact on the way our homes both look and function. All too often, however, storage is tackled as an afterthought, in a piecemeal fashion, when it should be part and parcel of the way we plan and conceive our homes as a whole. As time goes by and possessions accumulate, it becomes easier and easier to slip out of sync until what we own starts to get the upper hand.

Getting organized is necessarily a two-pronged attack. On the one hand it means planning efficient, accessible and workable systems for keeping the diverse range of belongings that the average home contains.

On the other hand, it means taking a long, hard, critical look at what you own and disposing of what is surplus to requirements. Our lives do not stand still and it is important to accept that this part of the process is fairly ongoing.

'A place for everything and everything in its place' has a rather joyless, worthy ring to it, but the simple truth is that without good systems of organization our homes become much less pleasant places to be. If you are constantly turning the house upside down looking for things, if you cannot carry out basic chores and routines without frustration, or if you regularly misplace important pieces of paperwork, you are adding an unnecessary degree of vexation into your everyday life.

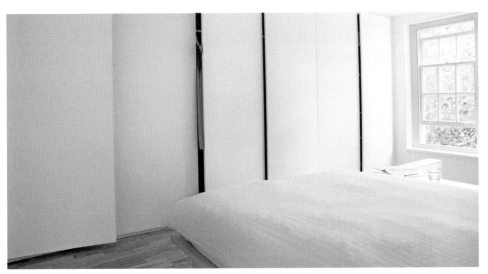

LEFT: OPEN CUBBYHOLES ABOVE A PREPARATION AREA KEEP A DIVERSE RANGE OF KITCHEN EQUIPMENT AND PROVISIONS CLOSE AT HAND.

ABOVE: THE BEDROOM SHOULD BE A SANCTUARY. SEAMLESS BUILT-IN CLOSETS WITH FLUSH DOORS HELP TO PRESERVE A MOOD OF RELAXATION.

continued

Introduction

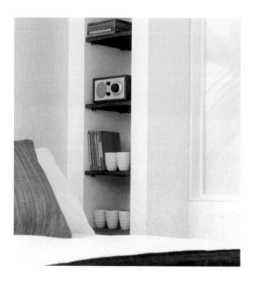

Clutter can also mean additional expense. Possessions and provisions that are not kept in proper conditions deteriorate and will require replacement sooner rather than later. Over-stuffed drawers and clothes rails invite moths to decimate your wardrobe. Refrigerators in dire need of defrosting do not keep fresh food at the optimum temperature. Items that disappear for good mean that you are forced to buy duplicates. When every nook and cranny is full to bursting, you will also find it harder to keep your home clean. Then there is the psychological impact to consider. When clutter is obscuring the picture,

ABOVE: CONCEALED SHELVING PROVIDES AN ALTERNATIVE TO A BEDSIDE TABLE WITH NEAT SLOTS FOR BOOKS AND A RADIO.

RIGHT: SHELVES CANTILEVERED FROM THE WALL ARE VISUALLY UNOBTRUSIVE. THE MINIMAL DETAILING SUITS THE CLEAN-LINED CONTEMPORARY SPACE.

you lose focus and concentration and everything seems to become an uphill struggle.

Adopting good storage systems is not about imposing an alien discipline on your lifestyle, but about making the most of the space at your disposal. These days, space is much more valuable than almost anything we keep in it. Hanging onto a lot of redundant clutter is a direct waste of money. What is worth more: the space itself or the kitchen gadget you never use? People sometimes feel that they need a bigger kitchen, or a bigger home, when what they really need to do is to get rid of all those things that they are keeping for no good reason.

How you organize your belongings should support and reflect the way you like to work, whether you are cooking a family meal or doing the laundry. If you like to stir-fry, for example, it makes sense to keep a wok with the rest of your pots and pans. If you do not use it very often, it belongs somewhere else. At the same time, a sense of order allows you the freedom to display those belongings that give you most satisfaction and derive real pleasure from your surroundings.

In the dim and distant past, most people owned so few possessions that a simple chest was generally sufficient for household storage. By the eighteenth century, specific types of storage furniture, such as sewing tables, secretaries and bookcases, began to appear to cater for increasing numbers and types of belongings. Today, there is a vast range of storage solutions from which to choose, from traditional freestanding furniture, to modular systems, to fitted and built-in units – everything to suit all tastes and budgets.

INTRODUCTION

PLANNING & ASSESSMENT

TYPES OF STORAGE

AREA BY AREA

Assessing your needs

When it comes to planning storage, the essential first step is to review both your possessions and the amount of space at your disposal. Changes of lifestyle or circumstance are natural points for rethinking storage arrangements on a broad scale. On the other hand, there are certain areas, such as routine household paperwork and accounts, where the process of review needs to be undertaken on a regular basis.

- Where are you feeling the pinch? Most people have particular places where clutter tends to build up. If you buy a lot of books and magazines, there will come a time when you will not have shelf space for all of them.
- Do you often lose things or waste time hunting for them? Good organization means thinking about accessibility so that what you need can be located easily.
- Do you regularly have to dispose of foodstuffs or other perishables before they are used up? Planning storage means thinking about your patterns of food consumption so that you do not over-buy.
- Are there areas in your home where possessions tend to accumulate? Stairs, hall tables and kitchen counters often serve as a kind of limbo for items that have no real home or which are being stored too remotely from where they are most often used.

ABOVE: A DEDICATED SHOE CUPBOARD FOR A DEDICATED FOLLOWER OF FASHION ORGANIZES LIKE WITH LIKE.

RIGHT: SHELVED BOOKS ARE EASY TO RETRIEVE AND LOOK ATTRACTIVE. IDEALLY, THEY SHOULD BE ORGANIZED ALPHABETICALLY AND/OR BY SUBJECT.

Life stages

We accumulate belongings at different rates according to our needs and circumstances. Natural times for thorough storage reviews include major transition points: setting up home with a partner, starting a family, moving house or children leaving home. Any home improvement project that entails some disruption, such as redecoration or building work, can also provide an ideal opportunity for a clear-out. Stripping a room of furnishings and possessions to allow painting to take place makes you view the space with fresh eyes.

- Most first homes tend to be on the small side. This is a stage where you might wish to think about hiring outside storage space until you can afford somewhere larger. It is also a time when there can be a certain amount of duplication, especially if you are moving in with a partner.
- Good systems of organization are vital for the family home. Children grow fast and acquire possessions at the speed of light. Regular clear-outs and flexible, accessible storage is key for smooth-running household routines.
- The empty nest can be surprisingly cluttered if you do not manage to persuade grown-up children to take their belongings with them. Now is a good time for a radical overhaul of possessions and spatial rearrangement.

ABOVE: CHILDREN LIKE TO SEE THEIR FAVOURITE POSSESSIONS OUT ON VIEW. DISPLAYING PICTURE BOOKS FACING OUTWARDS HELPS THEM TO MAKE A SELECTION WHEN IT COMES TO BEDTIME STORIES.

LEFT: A BEDROOM IN A CONVERTED ATTIC HAS BEEN FITTED OUT WITH SHELVES UNDER THE EAVES.

Reviewing your possessions

Clutter is a subjective notion. Some people naturally tend towards the 'less is more' end of the spectrum, others are inveterate hoarders. Most of us, however, are somewhere in the middle, conscious that there are certain areas of our home organization that could do with improvement. Getting to grips with your possessions means asking yourself a series of basic questions: Is it worth keeping? Is it worth repairing? Where is best to put it?

Our relationship with our belongings can be surprisingly emotional. While most people have no sentimental attachment to basic kit, such as tin-openers or toothbrushes, it is often hard to part with more personal things, even if they are worn out, under used or redundant in some other way. Guilt also plays a part, particularly if the item in question was expensive. Here it is important to remember that hanging onto a bad buy will not redeem the purchase.

De-junking not only frees up space, it has other positive advantages as well. A clutter-free home is easier to clean and maintain. It allows you room to display and take pleasure in your favourite possessions and it generally promotes a relaxed frame of mind.

LEFT: CLEARING OUT THE CLUTTER LEAVES YOU ROOM TO DISPLAY WHAT YOU REALLY LOVE. THIS CABINET HOUSES A COLLECTION OF RETRO CHINA.

RIGHT: PROPPING UP PICTURES, RATHER THAN HANGING THEM, MEANS THAT YOU ARE NOT COMMITTED TO A PERMANENT ARRANGEMENT AND YOU CAN VARY THE DISPLAY FROM TIME TO TIME.

Getting rid of things

- Work systematically through a category of possessions, such as your wardrobe or your filing cabinet, and set aside enough time to complete the job.

- Get rid of anything you have not worn or used for a year (except those items, such as Christmas decorations or catering size dishes that only see seasonal use).

- Most duplicate items, including CDs, books and kitchen or garden tools, should be disposed of. Keep the newest or the one that works the best.

- Remove from your wardrobe any item of clothing that does not fit or does not suit you.

- Consider disposing of anything that has been sitting around for months waiting for repair – the chances are that you do not need it.

- Weed out equipment, materials or supplies that relate to activities that you no longer pursue or never got round to taking up.

- Impulse buys and 'bargains' that you later regretted, unwanted gifts, unread books are all guilt-inducing and do not deserve house room.

- Cast a critical eye over perishable items and get rid of those past their sell-by date. Even preserves, tinned food and dried herbs cannot be kept indefinitely.

- Cosmetics, medicines, paints, chemicals and insecticides often linger on well past their shelf life. Many of these items require specialist disposal.

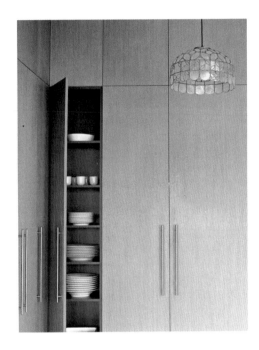

ABOVE: STORE PLATES AND BOWLS IN SMALL MANAGEABLE STACKS ORGANIZED BY SIZE AND TYPE. CRACKED AND CHIPPED CROCKERY IS UNHYGIENIC AND SHOULD BE DISCARDED.

LEFT: TO KEEP KITCHEN SHELVES IN ORDER, CHECK LABELS ON A REGULAR BASIS TO MAKE SURE THAT YOU ARE NOT KEEPING ANYTHING PAST ITS USE-BY DATE.

Recycling & disposal

Donations to charity

- Donate only what is clean and in good condition, otherwise you are just passing on the problem to someone else.
- Do not leave donations outside the shop between opening hours.
- Think about local hospitals, schools, libraries and clinics as well as charity shops – they often welcome second-hand toys, books, magazines and CDs.
- Some local areas will collect bulkier items that are less easy to dispose of.

Recycling

- Take the time to sort your rubbish for either doorstep collection or removal to a recycling bank or centre.
- Some local schemes will collect and repair furniture and electrical appliances, offering them for sale to low-income households.
- Internet swap-shops or free-cycle sites allow you to exchange things you do not want for things that you do.

Selling

- If you do not know the value of a particular item, you may need expert opinion before offering it for sale.
- Outlets range from car boot and garage sales, to auction houses, second-hand outlets and eBay. Auctions are the best way to dispose of items that are difficult to price or those that have greater intrinsic value.

Throwing away

- Consult your local council about the right way to dispose of chemicals, batteries and the like.
- Shred all documents that include details of your identity and banking arrangements.

ABOVE: PIECES OF VINTAGE CHINA MAY BE COLLECTABLE. IT MAY BE WORTH CHECKING THE VALUE OF SOME ITEMS BEFORE YOU DISPOSE OF THEM.

RIGHT: BRIGHTLY COLOURED METAL BINS HELP YOU TO SORT HOUSEHOLD RUBBISH FOR DOORSTEP COLLECTION.

Levels of storage

Clutter is not simply having too much stuff; it is having stuff in the wrong place. Once you have got rid of everything that is surplus to requirements, think about where you are currently keeping things. Accessibility and frequency of use are the two key factors to consider.

At hand

Anything that you use on a daily basis should be stored close at hand in the area where it will be used. In many cases, that means out on view, hanging from racks or rails, or stored on open shelves within reaching distance.

Possessions to keep close at hand

- Essential cooking ingredients and utensils. The kitchen is one area where you need to be able to reach for things instinctively at a moment's notice. Whatever you keep on hand should reflect what you like to eat and how you cook.
- Pending paperwork, including bills and other household accounts. Keep these separate from other correspondence. Family calendars, school notices and homework fall into the same category.
- Personal care products, such as toothpaste, toothbrushes, soaps and shampoos.
- Items required rarely but acutely, such as first aid boxes, spare fuses and light bulbs. Never lock a first aid box. Keep it out of the reach of children, but in an accessible place.

LEFT: BATH PRODUCTS THAT YOU USE ON A DAILY BASIS SHOULD BE KEPT OUT ON VIEW AS CLOSE TO THE BATHTUB OR SHOWER AS POSSIBLE.

FAR LEFT: THE COFFEE TABLE IS A CONVENIENT PLACE TO KEEP REMOTE CONTROLS, LISTINGS GUIDES AND BOOKS. THIS ONE HAS INTERNAL STORAGE SPACE.

continued

Levels of storage

Nearby

Most household provisions and belongings are used regularly but intermittently. These need to be stored near where they will be required, but out of the main areas of activity. Keep a close eye on how often such items are used. If they rarely see an outing, think about getting rid of them completely or storing them in a less accessible place.

Think about how you actually use particular areas in your home. If you listen to music in the kitchen, for example, it makes sense to provide a place for storing CDs.

Possessions to keep nearby

- Cooking ingredients, condiments and provisions that you use weekly or monthly rather than daily, including foodstuffs you buy in bulk. Review these periodically to check they are not past their use-by dates.
- Cooking equipment, dishes and utensils with more specialized functions. Think about the way you cook. If you cook a lot of stir-fries, it makes sense to keep a wok close at hand, but if not, store it away from the main cooking and preparation area.
- Spare linen and bedding.
- Books, files and documents to which you regularly refer, as opposed to those that relate to your career history.
- Best or second sets of china, glassware and tableware.
- Clothing and outdoor wear that are appropriate to the season.

ABOVE: KEEP KITCHEN WORKTOPS CLEAR WITH WELL-ORGANIZED STORAGE. ARRANGE CUPBOARD CONTENTS ACCORDING TO FREQUENCY OF USE.

RIGHT: THE SAME PRINCIPLE HOLDS TRUE FOR BOOKSHELVES. KEEP BOOKS TO WHICH YOU OFTEN REFER WITHIN EASY REACH.

continued

Levels of storage

Deep storage

The best places for deep storage are attics, basements, garages and any out-of-the-way locations, including rented storage facilities. Make sure that conditions are adequate and that there is no risk of damage from moths, mice or damp.

Store your possessions in sturdy, rigid, lidded containers. Label what you put away and keep a list so that you know what you have stored and where it is. Any clothing that you pack away for long periods should be clean, folded between layers of acid-free tissue and zipped into garment bags. These should be kept at a stable level of humidity, away from direct sunlight.

Never consign something to deep storage to avoid making a decision about whether you should keep it or not. By the same token, renting outside storage space can be expensive. Consider whether the items you are storing are worth the rental fees.

Possessions to keep in deep storage

- Out-of-season items of clothing and sports kit, such as skiing equipment or wetsuits.
- Christmas decorations.
- Any large pans or serving dishes that are used very infrequently.
- Records such as tax returns that must be kept for legal reasons, along with sentimental items, such as children's artwork, that form part of your personal family archive.
- Hand-me-down children's clothing and toys.
- Suitcases, bags and rucksacks – unless you travel frequently.

LEFT: HIGH SHELVES AND STACKED BOXES ARE GOOD STORAGE SOLUTIONS FOR BOOKS AND OTHER ITEMS THAT YOU DO NOT USE ON A REGULAR BASIS.

RIGHT: A WALL OF BUILT-IN CUPBOARDS PROVIDES A STOWING PLACE FOR A WIDE RANGE OF BELONGINGS. USE HIGH-LEVEL CUPBOARDS FOR DEEP STORAGE.

Ergonomics

Ergonomics is the study of the relationship between workers and their environment. Successful ergonomic design should reduce discomfort and prevent repetitive strain injury. In storage terms, ergonomics suggests optimum heights and depths for shelving, worktops and cupboards. Such considerations are most critical in hard-working areas, such as kitchens, where a range of activities must be performed comfortably, safely and efficiently.

- Reach is a key factor. Anything that you use regularly should be kept between waist and eye level. This applies as much to books and files as it does to kitchen provisions and cooking equipment.
- High-level storage, accessed by a ladder or stool, should be devoted to lighter, less bulky items that are required infrequently.
- Heavy items can cause back strain when you are retrieving them. They should be stored at waist level or just below.
- Bear in mind that bending down takes up more space than reaching up. Similarly, if space is tight, consider replacing cupboard or unit doors that open outwards with those that slide across.
- Do not overfill containers to the point where you cannot shift them without assistance. This is particularly relevant for items that you keep in deep storage. A number of modular, labelled containers that can be stacked neatly is better than a single heavy trunk.

ABOVE: ESSENTIAL SHOWER ITEMS ARE STORED ON HANGING METAL SHELVING FOR EASY RETRIEVAL.

RIGHT: THE ALCOVES TO EITHER SIDE OF A CHIMNEY BREAST ARE NATURAL PLACES FOR FITTED STORAGE. WICKER BASKETS MAKE IDEAL CONTAINERS FOR LINEN AND LAUNDRY, AS THEY ALLOW AIR TO CIRCULATE.

INTRODUCTION

PLANNING & ASSESSMENT

TYPES OF STORAGE

AREA BY AREA

Basic considerations

How and where you keep your possessions defines the overall appearance of your home to a far greater degree than any other element. If possible, storage should be planned early on in the design process, rather than tackled as an afterthought once your belongings have started to accumulate.

There are three broad types of storage: fitted, unfitted and out on view. In practice, most homes contain a mixture of all three, with the balance varying according to individual taste and the amount of space you have. Within each category, it is possible to express almost any decorative approach or style, from sleek and contemporary to rustic or traditional.

ABOVE: FREESTANDING STORAGE FURNITURE, SUCH AS WARDROBES, CHESTS AND OTHER CONTAINERS, PRESENT ANOTHER BASIC STORAGE APPROACH.

LEFT: ROBUST, CATERING-STYLE METAL SHELVING AND PULL-OUT TRAYS HAVE BEEN USED TO CUSTOMIZE THE INTERIOR OF THIS FITTED KITCHEN.

- Think about the whole picture to ensure that you are using all the space at your disposal to the optimum degree.
- Landings, hallways and stairs can make useful storage areas when fitted out with shelving or seamless cupboards. Most homes have hidden corners or under-used areas that can be exploited in a similar fashion.
- Reconsider room allocation. When children are small and play is floor-based, it makes sense for them to share the largest bedroom. If you have a separate dining room, but rarely eat there, it may be better used for some other family activity.
- Think about converting redundant attics, basements or other spaces into fully fledged rooms, easing the pressure on the rest of your home. Alternatively, they can be turned into storage areas with a few simple adjustments.

Shelving

Shelving is an affordable and versatile way of organizing clutter in every area of the home. A vast number of items can be shelved, from books and magazines to CDs, clothing, games, crockery and glassware.

- Shelving works best when it is conceived wholeheartedly. A few shelves dotted around will not supply much in the way of storage space and will look untidy.
- Plan ahead: think about what you are going to put on the shelves and adjust the height and depth accordingly. It is worth allowing a generous margin for future acquisitions.
- Alcove shelving makes use of the recesses to either side of the chimney breast. You can extend shelves from floor to ceiling or combine upper shelves with closed cupboards lower down for those items you do not want to see on display.
- An entire wall lined with shelves is visually neat. You can extend the shelving around and above doorways and windows for a solid, architectural effect.
- Low perimeter shelving at a level below waist height suits contemporary spaces, especially those with a strong horizontal emphasis and where the ceiling is relatively low.
- Paint shelving the same colour as the walls to make it less intrusive.

ABOVE: SHELVING ALWAYS LOOKS MORE CONSIDERED IF IT IS TAILORED TO THE DIMENSIONS OF WHAT YOU KEEP THERE. HERE, THE SPINES OF CDS AND RECORDS MAKE AN ATTRACTIVE GRAPHIC DISPLAY.

RIGHT: A WORKING WALL OF SHELVES ORGANIZES AN ENTIRE LIBRARY WITHOUT LOOKING CLUTTERED. PLAN SHELVING SO THAT IT READS AS PART OF THE FABRIC OF THE ROOM.

continued

Shelving

Practical considerations

- For most wooden shelves, including those made of softwood or MDF, the recommended span between supports should be no greater than 700mm (27$\frac{1}{2}$in) for heavy loads, such as books. You can decrease the span slightly for lighter loads.
- Flexible shelving systems are widely available. These consist of vertical wood or metal supports and some form of bracketing to hold shelves. In practice, most people tend not to adjust shelving once it is up, but such systems do allow you to experiment with spacing.
- Cantilevered shelves, where the means of support is hidden, are ideal for display.
- It is important to make sure that the wall or walls can bear the weight of both the shelving and its load. You will need to use rawl plugs and counter-sunk screws to attach built-in shelving. Some additional means of anchorage is also recommended for freestanding bookcases, particularly if the floor is not perfectly level.
- Shelves made of manufactured wood, such as MDF, have raw edges. These can be concealed behind a thin softwood batten. The battens will also provide extra rigidity and bracing.
- Arrange shelving so that deeper shelves spaced farther apart are at the lower levels. These can take heavy or bulky items. Higher up, shelves can be more tightly spaced or shallower. A comfortable visual break between the two is about one-third up the wall, at dado height.

ABOVE: CUSTOM-MADE NARROW SHELVING UNITS ARE BRACED AT THE TOP FOR STABILITY. ALWAYS ENSURE BOOKCASES ARE SECURELY ANCHORED.

LEFT: AN ARRAY OF WHITE METAL CANTILEVERED SHELVES HOUSES A MUSIC COLLECTION. THERE ARE MANY WELL-DESIGNED SYSTEMS ON THE MARKET.

Hanging

All homes need some hanging space, most of which will be devoted to clothing. Coats, suits, dresses, shirts, skirts and trousers are best stored hanging up to prevent creases.

- The depth of hanging space is a critical issue. Allow at least 600mm (24in) to provide easy access to clothing and to prevent them from getting crumpled.
- Hanging rails should be long enough to move clothes around freely – overstuffed closets and rails encourage moths and crush clothes. Allow a margin for new acquisitions.
- Double-hanging, where rails are arranged one above the other, makes an efficient use of space. Items such as jackets, shirts and skirts can be double-hung, with a separate hanging rail for full-length dresses and coats. Alternatively, the area underneath a rail can be fitted with shelves, drawers or trays for storing folded clothes and shoes.
- It is useful to arrange hanging space so that clothes of a similar type, length or colour are grouped together.
- Invest in decent hangers. Avoid using wire hangers except for shirts you wear frequently. Wooden hangers help clothes to keep their shape and padded hangers are best for delicate items.
- Hang skirts from tape loops or use sprung or clip hangers.
- Provide low hanging rails for small children to encourage them to dress themselves.

ABOVE: DOUBLE-HANGING MAKES AN EFFICIENT USE OF SPACE IN A FITTED WARDROBE AND ALLOWS YOU TO GROUP CLOTHING OF A SIMILAR LENGTH AND TYPE.

RIGHT: HANGING FABRIC TIDIES ARE USEFUL FOR STORING CLOTHES AND SHOES IN A VISIBLE WAY. LIKEWISE WITH CLEAR PLASTIC CONTAINERS.

continued

Hanging

Options

- The open clothes rail has proved a popular way of providing hanging space. However, it can be visually intrusive in a bedroom and it also exposes clothes to fading from sunlight and to dust. It is better to use clothes rails only for capsule wardrobes and keep the rest of your clothing in more protected surroundings.
- Freestanding wardrobes, which tend to devour space and dominate the bedroom, are less popular than they once were, but they can be a good solution for storing a limited number of clothes and they are often very affordable. Ideally, they should be sited in alcoves or recesses.

- Fitted clothes storage varies widely in style and quality, from mass-market versions that can be customized according to your needs to high-end bespoke solutions. Wherever possible, it is best to devote an entire wall to clothes storage, and incorporate hanging or shelving space within it.
- To protect against sunlight and dust, screen hanging storage with doors or panels. If space is an issue consider using blinds or sliding, bifolding or concertina doors.
- Pocketed mesh tubes suspended from the ceiling make an accessible way of storing children's toys and possessions.

FAR LEFT: THIS BUILT-IN CLOSET FOR OUTDOOR WEAR IS IMMEDIATELY ADJACENT TO THE MAIN ENTRANCE. AN INTERIOR LIGHT IS AN ASSET.

LEFT: DEEP PULL-OUT CUPBOARDS WITH HANGING RAILS HAVE BEEN NEATLY INTEGRATED INTO THE SPACE UNDERNEATH A HIGH-LEVEL BED.

Racks & rails

Racks, rails, pegboards and hooks are variations of hanging storage and are ideal for organizing specific categories of possessions: keys and kitchen equipment, belts and ties, tools and bicycles. These are chiefly utilitarian solutions for workrooms, kitchens and out-of-the-way locations.

- Ensure that the means of suspension – wire, rod, rail or rack – is strong enough to bear the weight of the items you will be hanging from it and is securely anchored to the wall or ceiling.
- It is relatively simple to rig up a rack or rail using equipment from a hardware store. Alternatively, DIY outlets and kitchen and bathroom retailers offer a number of basic racking systems to help you make the most of your wall space.
- Heavy duty wall or ceiling brackets that are specifically designed for hanging up bicycles, lawnmowers and other bulky gear are also widely available – just check what weight your wall or ceiling can bear first.
- Hooks and pegs tend to look best when they are grouped together in a line, rather than dotted about here and there. A single hook or peg placed on the back of a bathroom or bedroom door, for example, will quickly become overloaded.

ABOVE: BASIC COOKING UTENSILS HANGING FROM HOOKS MAKE A PRACTICAL AND SCULPTURAL WORKING DISPLAY IN THE KITCHEN.

RIGHT: ROBUST KITCHEN HANGING RAILS CAN BE USED TO SUSPEND A WIDE RANGE OF ITEMS, FROM ROLLS OF PAPER TOWEL TO SAUCEPANS.

continued

Racks & rails

Options

- A row of Shaker-style pegs or hooks in a lower hallway is a good way of organizing outdoor gear if you do not have a convenient closet. It provides far more hanging space than the average freestanding coat stand.

- Hanging racks and rails can make a positive contribution to the visual appeal of the kitchen. Utensils, pans, colanders and other items of basic equipment look attractive suspended over the preparation area where they are conveniently to hand. Make sure that what you display is in regular use, otherwise you will have to clean items more often than you would need to if they were stored in closed cupboards.

- Heated towel rails provide a good way of storing and warming bath linen. In a small bathroom they may supply all the heating you need.

- You can make use of the backs of wardrobe or cupboard doors to hang up ties and belts, or to store pan lids and cleaning utensils.

- Racks and rails are an ideal solution for organizing tools in a workshop, shed or utility room. Use hooks or brackets to suspend tools from a perforated pegboard. Drawing or painting the outline of the tool on the board makes it easier to keep everything in its place, and reminds you when friends or family have borrowed something.

ABOVE: A WALL-MOUNTED PLATE RACK POSITIONED NEAR A SINK ALLOWS DISHES TO DRAIN DRY.

LEFT: AN OLD WOODEN LADDER MAKES AN IMPROVIZED RACKING SYSTEM FOR A COLLECTION OF MAGAZINES.

Storage units

Storage units occupy something of a middle ground between fully fitted or built-in storage and traditional storage furniture. Like storage furniture, they are freestanding and do not commit you to a permanent arrangement, but their relative anonymity makes them less conspicuous. Many units are available as part of a modular system, which means that you can add extra capacity later on or configure an arrangement according to your needs, combining, for example, open shelves or cubbyholes with closed cabinets and drawers. At the most minimal are simple cubes that can be stacked into a tower or arranged to form a storage wall. As mobile elements, storage units are also a good solution if you do not expect to be in your present home very long.

Aside from their prime function as storage space, these types of modular units can be a good way of providing a degree of separation in a multipurpose or open-plan space. A storage unit placed at right angles to the wall can provide an element of enclosure to screen a kitchen area or to separate an eating or study area from a more general living space. Unlike solid partitions, storage units will not block light and views, particularly if you use them chiefly for display.

ABOVE: THIS WALL-MOUNTED MODULAR STORAGE SYSTEM COMBINES OPEN CUBBYHOLES WITH CLOSED CABINETS BELOW.

RIGHT: A MODULAR STORAGE UNIT ON CASTORS DOUBLES UP AS A MEANS OF PARTITIONING SPACE WITHOUT BLOCKING LIGHT.

continued

Storage units

Points to consider

- When choosing a storage unit or modular system you must ensure that it is robust enough to do its job properly. Cheaper units tend to be flimsy and easily tipped over without some additional form of wall anchorage. Look out for designs that have good cross bracing for extra rigidity.

- Reclaimed or new steel, or steel wire storage systems, designed for commercial or retail purposes, are very strong and stable. Many are anonymous enough to work in living areas as well as behind-the-scenes locations.

- Mobile units, such trolleys and those fitted with castors, add flexibility to spatial arrangements. These can be particularly useful for kitchen and bathroom storage, tucking away under a counter when not required. Some mobile kitchen units incorporate chopping blocks on the top for extra counter space.

- As well as large storage units, there are numerous smaller designs intended for more specific uses. Modular racks and cases designed to accommodate CDs are a case in point. In many homes, collections of CDs and DVDs are ever-expanding. A modular system can be added to as need arises and will be visually neater than a random collection of different racks or towers.

ABOVE: A MOBILE WOODEN DRAWER UNIT IS A HANDSOME VARIATION ON THE THEME OF THE TROLLEY.

LEFT: SIMPLICITY IS A DEFINING ELEMENT OF MANY CONTEMPORARY STORAGE UNITS, WHICH MEANS THEY CAN BE USED ALMOST ANYWHERE IN THE HOME.

Fitted storage

Fitted storage ranges from mass-market units for kitchens, bathrooms or wardrobes to bespoke designs constructed for a specific context. Although some of the floor area may need to be sacrificed, fitted storage often represents the best solution for small spaces, particularly small kitchens and bathrooms, where there are fixed servicing points in the layout. Installing fitted storage requires precise planning and expert construction to fit properly and look good.

Planning fitted storage

Whether you are buying off-the-peg units or commissioning someone to build closets and cupboards for you, the first step is to plan everything on paper.

- Make a rough sketch of the area or areas in question. If you have extensive storage needs, plot out your entire home so that you can consider different solutions.
- It is very important to take detailed, accurate measurements. Even small errors of calculation make a difference.
- Use your measurements to draw up a scale plan. Work on graph paper and add existing features, such as windows, doors, servicing points, sockets and switches.
- Take the plan along to an in-store design service or use it to form the basis of discussions with a builder.
- Think about the dimensions and quantity of what you intend to store.
- Bear in mind that cupboard doors and drawers will need clearance in front for easy access.

ABOVE: FITTED STORAGE CAN BE BEAUTIFULLY TAILORED TO YOUR EXACT REQUIREMENTS.

RIGHT: A FITTED SOLUTION WORKS IN MANY AREAS OF THE HOME, NOT JUST KITCHENS AND BATHROOMS.

continued

Fitted storage

Design & construction

- Pay attention to proportion and scale. You can extend fitted cupboards to the full height of a room, for example, rather than stopping short of the ceiling. In older properties, treat alcoves to either side of the chimney breast in the same way.

- Make sure that the position of fitted units in kitchens and bathrooms does not prevent you from accessing servicing such as stop cocks.

- For the most minimal effect, use flush doors and panels that open on press catches and paint them the same colour as the walls.

- For a lighter effect, screen fitted units or cupboards with semi-transparent doors or drawer fronts made of Perspex or plastic. Backlighting can also be very effective.

- The basic carcass of fitted units can be constructed in a relatively cheap material, which will leave you more money to spend on doors, panels and drawer fronts.

- Do not be tempted to tackle the work yourself unless you are entirely confident of your abilities. Flat-pack kitchens and bathrooms can be tricky to install. Many stores now provide a design service (if you supply the measurements) and will also handle the installation for you.

- If your storage needs are complex and involve spatial planning, it is often best to engage the services of a designer or architect.

ABOVE: LIGHTING CONCEALED AT THE TOP OF FITTED CUPBOARDS WASHES A BEDROOM CEILING WITH A GENTLE GLOW, CONTRIBUTING TO AN AURA OF CALM.

LEFT: BRUSHED STAINLESS STEEL UNIT DOORS TURN A WALL OF FITTED KITCHEN STORAGE INTO A CONTEMPORARY LIGHT-REFLECTING FEATURE.

Customizing fitted storage

Bear in mind that whether you are buying mass-produced fitted units from a major retail chain or paying a specialist retailer or contractor to construct built-in storage, you are literally buying space. In most cases you will find that you need to customize the interiors of cupboards and drawers in some fashion to make the most of your investment. Most fitted units come in standard modules and one size will not necessarily be suitable for all your needs.

- Many retailers supply a range of accessories, from inset racks to drawer dividers to help you use storage space to its fullest extent.
- Movable shelves allow you to adapt the interior space to accommodate items of different heights so that no room is wasted.
- Carousel units avoid dead areas in the corners of kitchen layouts.
- Tidies, racks and other types of organizer can be hung on the back of cupboard doors to keep like with like.
- Ease of retrieval is an important consideration. If your fitted storage is extensive and minimally detailed, you may not always remember where certain items are stored. A sketch plan or inventory can be an asset.
- For deep cupboards, larders and walk-in wardrobes, you will need artificial lighting of some kind so you can see what is in the farthest recesses. Information lights that are triggered by the opening of a door are adequate for most small closets or cupboards. Larger storage areas will require proper switchable lights.

LEFT: PULL-OUT PANTRY OR LARDER CUPBOARDS ALLOW YOU TO SEE EXACTLY WHAT PROVISIONS YOU HAVE AT A GLANCE.

RIGHT: WOODEN SUPPORTS IN DEEP DRAWERS ALLOW STACKS OF CROCKERY TO BE HELD FIRMLY IN PLACE WITHOUT THE RISK OF SCRATCHING OR CHIPPING.

Storage furniture

Storage furniture encompasses a wide variety of options and designs, from dressers and chests of drawers to sideboards and bookcases. Style varies too, from characterful period pieces to clean-lined contemporary reinterpretations in sleek modern materials.

Many types of storage furniture, such as chests and chests of drawers, are versatile enough to house a variety of possessions. Others, such as filing cabinets, are more specific. If you do not expect to stay in your present home very long or are unable to alter it, such pieces are a sensible investment, as you can take them with you when you move.

One disadvantage of storage furniture is that it takes up more floor space than fitted units or cupboards. Large pieces can crowd a room uncomfortably. A bed, for example, is a dominant piece of furniture in its own right. Once you add a freestanding wardrobe and a chest of drawers into the equation, you might find it difficult to move comfortably around your bedroom.

A related disadvantage is that buying another piece of storage furniture to solve all your storage requirements can result in a rather haphazard design effect. Plan ahead and think about how best you can meet your needs with a combination of both fitted and unfitted elements.

LEFT: ANTIQUE PIECES, SUCH AS THIS OLD GLASS-FRONTED WOODEN CABINET, PROVIDE VERSATILE AND ATTRACTIVE STORAGE PLACES.

ABOVE: STYLISH MID-TWENTIETH-CENTURY MODERN FURNITURE, DESIGNED FOR THE SMALLER HOME, IS LESS DOMINANT THAN OLDER DESIGNS.

continued

Storage furniture

Options

- Traditional pieces of storage furniture, such as the kitchen dresser, retain their popularity today and can form an attractive and practical centrepiece, both in period homes and more contemporary surroundings. Into the same category fall retro pieces such as maid-savers, which can add charm and wit to an interior.

- Contemporary versions of storage furniture are simpler, less monumental and come in a range of finishes and materials apart from wood. The sideboard, for example, has been reinvented as a long horizontal cabinet, which is useful for storing a range of items in a multipurpose space.

- Storage furniture originally designed for non-domestic contexts, such as retail display fittings, school lockers, old wooden filing cabinets and plan chests, can introduce a note of originality to your storage arrangements. These types of salvage pieces look particularly good in large open-plan areas, where their scale does not dominate.

- The need for space-saving solutions has seen a trend towards multipurpose furniture. Storage room is now incorporated into items such as beds, which have drawers in the base, or benches, which have lift-up seats with room for storage underneath.

ABOVE: TRADITIONAL DRESSERS AND OLD-FASHIONED CUPBOARDS CAN MAKE AN ARRESTING FOCAL POINT IN AN OTHERWISE FITTED KITCHEN.

RIGHT: IN RECENT YEARS, THE SIDEBOARD HAS MADE A COMEBACK, REINVENTED AS A VERSATILE CONTEMPORARY PIECE OF STORAGE FURNITURE THAT IS IDEAL FOR MULTIPURPOSE LIVING AREAS.

Containers

From cardboard boxes to glass jars, containers of various kinds are one of the main building blocks of home organization. Storing things in containers keeps them both safe and segregated. Grouping like with like is a basic storage principle.

Using containers is one of the cheapest ways of organizing your home and if you find clutter building up in a particular area you can respond almost immediately. A quick trip to the stationers to buy a set of box files, for example, can help you get to grips with your paperwork sooner rather than later. Since many shortfalls in home

organization are the result of procrastination, this approach has much to recommend it.

Containers represent storage on the level of detail and should be tailored to suit the appropriate items. You cannot apply the same solution across the board. By the same token, any container that is simply used as a dumping ground for a number of disparate items is not contributing to any system of organization and may make extra work. If you store your children's toys in a single large basket, the contents will simply get tipped onto the floor everytime they hunt for the toy they want to play with.

LEFT: WOVEN RATTAN BOXES LINED UP UNDER THE BATHROOM SINK HOUSE SPARE TOILET ROLLS, LINEN AND CLEANING PRODUCTS.

ABOVE: EVEN SMALL CONTAINERS ARE AN EFFECTIVE AND IMMEDIATE STORAGE SOLUTION IF YOU GROUP ITEMS OF THE SAME TYPE.

continued

Containers

Points to consider

- Scale is important. Keep small things in small containers or in containers within containers. Larger items or provisions you use in bulk need to be kept in larger containers.
- Containers that are out on view should have some sort of visual consistency, whether they are kitchen storage jars, plastic or metal boxes, or wicker baskets.
- Improvise by recycling food jars and tins, shoeboxes and other forms of packaging. Glass jars allow you to read their contents at a glance; other containers may need labels.
- Colour coding containers is a good way of sorting children's possessions or distinguishing between items that belong to different people.
- Do not store valuable items in locked boxes. A box with a lock tells a thief that the contents are worth stealing. If you must store valuable items at home, you should invest in a proper safe. Better still, rent a safe deposit box.
- Containers can be a useful way of organizing the contents of drawers or cupboards.
- Characterful old hat boxes, trunks and luggage can make quirky containers and look attractive on display.
- Rigid, lidded containers made of plastic are ideal for protecting items in deep storage.

ABOVE: FOR ORGANIZATION BEHIND THE SCENES, THERE IS A WIDE VARIETY OF CONTAINERS ON THE MARKET, SUCH AS THESE SMART, PLAIN BOXES WITH REINFORCED CORNERS.

RIGHT: CONTAINERS ARE INDISPENSABLE IN CHILDREN'S ROOMS AND ARE A GOOD WAY OF KEEPING ONE CHILD'S TOYS SEPARATE FROM ANOTHER'S.

Using redundant space

When every room is full to bursting point, it may not seem as if there is much space going spare. But most homes have hidden corners or out-of-the-way areas that can be adapted for storage, easing the pressure all round.

Converting attics & basements

You do not have to convert an attic or a basement into a habitable room to benefit from the additional floor area it provides. In the case of an attic, all you need to do is to cover the joists with a serviceable floor (hardboard will do) and provide a sturdy means of access. A light will also help. This type of minimal conversion will allow an attic to be used for deep storage. A basement also makes a good storage area. The cool dark conditions are actually beneficial for certain types of provision, such as wine.

- Pack items away in rigid lidded boxes and keep an inventory of what they contain.
- Attic joists are not as strong as floor joists on lower levels and you must be careful about weight. If you need to store really heavy items, you will need to strengthen the joists.
- If you plan to use a basement for storage, make sure that it is not damp.

ABOVE: THIS ATTIC HAS BEEN CONVERTED INTO A HOME OFFICE WHICH IS QUIETLY TUCKED OUT OF THE WAY OF THE REST OF THE HOUSEHOLD.

LEFT: THE STEPPED AREA UNDERNEATH THE STAIRS HAS INSPIRED A WIDE RANGE OF STORAGE SOLUTIONS, BOTH FITTED AND UNFITTED.

continued

Using redundant space

Stairways, halls & landings

The circulation spaces of stairways, halls and landings can make very useful storage areas. Rather than allow such spaces to silt up with clutter, fit them out properly with shelving, built-in cupboards or cubbyholes.

Take the opportunity to consider basic traffic routes around the home. If there are two doors providing access to a given area, one entrance will probably be favoured over the other. Blocking up a redundant doorway can win you more wall space for shelving or kitchen units.

- Wide hallways can be shelved floor to ceiling to house a library of books or files. Alternatively you can line one wall with fitted cupboards to take outdoor clothing.

- Wall or ceiling brackets can be used to rack bicycles in a back hallway.
- Generous landings can accommodate extra storage, either built-in or freestanding. A chest, for example, can be used to store spare towels, bed linen or extra quilts, with the top doubling up as a display area.
- The staggered space below a staircase can be easily adapted to house a wide range of items. For an unfitted approach, you can use containers or storage units of varying heights. Built-in shelving, cupboards and drawers, however, will provide a more seamless and integrated solution.
- Custom-designed stairs can be detailed to provide storage caches either underneath or between the treads.

ABOVE: HERE, LARGE DRAWERS HAVE BEEN NEATLY SLOTTED INTO A RAISED PLATFORM TO PROVIDE ADDITIONAL STORAGE SPACE.

RIGHT: A COMPACT HOME OFFICE OCCUPIES THE STAGGERED SPACE BELOW A FLIGHT OF STAIRS. THE SLIMLINE RADIATOR IS AN EFFECTIVE SPACE-SAVER.

Display

Those possessions that you keep out on view should either contribute to your enjoyment of your surroundings or be in constant use. In some cases, they can do both. Working displays of kitchen utensils or bowls of fresh fruit and vegetables are practical as well as aesthetically pleasing. Shelves of books have an attractive rhythmic patterning.

Natural areas for display include mantelpieces, tables and desktops, as well as shelving, storage units and walls. Circulation spaces such as stairways, halls and landings can also be good places for display. Here, pictures and decorative objects add character to what can otherwise be somewhat featureless parts of the home.

- Allow plenty of breathing space around the objects that you put out on display so that they can be fully appreciated.
- Take the trouble to change your displays from time to time to give yourself something fresh to look at.
- Display only what you are prepared to look after and make sure that it will not be damaged by exposure to light.
- Accent lighting will add an extra quality to decorative display: the delicate transparency of glass can be accentuated by backlighting, sidelighting emphasizes form and texture, and highlighting a single object with a narrow beam will create drama.

FAR LEFT: COLLECTIONS OF OBJECTS UNITED BY TYPE, COLOUR OR FORM HAVE MORE IMPACT THAN THE SAME OBJECTS DOTTED ABOUT FROM PLACE TO PLACE.

LEFT: DISPLAY SHELVES AT HIGH LEVEL PROVIDE A STRONG VISUAL CONNECTION BETWEEN TWO ROOMS THAT HAVE BEEN KNOCKED TOGETHER.

continued

Display

Collections

Many people are drawn to collecting, even if what they collect has little intrinsic value. By its very nature, a collection is when quantity becomes a quality in itself.

- The golden rule for displaying collections is to group objects together in one place or otherwise contain them in some way, for example, within a frame, in a display cabinet or ranged on a dresser. Grouping lends impact and allows the collection to be read as a whole. A collection that is dotted around the place is simply clutter.
- Group objects according to theme, colour, pattern or some other unifying element.
- Variations in height can be very effective.
- For small collections, odd numbers – threes, fives and sevens – are visually more appealing than even numbers.

Pictures

- Rather than dot pictures and framed photographs about the place, devote one wall to display, or hang one picture prominently. Leave the remaining walls clear to provide breathing space.
- A collection of small pictures of a similar type, such as prints or photographs, look most effective hung in a group. If they are all the same size, arrange them in orderly rows, but if not, experiment with different arrangements by laying them out on the floor and seeing what looks best.

ABOVE: AN IMPROMPTU COLLAGE OF POSTCARDS, PHOTOGRAPHS AND CLIPPINGS PROVIDES INSPIRATION ABOVE A WORKTABLE.

RIGHT: GROUP COLLECTIONS WITHIN SOME SORT OF FRAMEWORK SO THAT THEY READ AS A WHOLE. THESE WHITE PAINTED CANTILEVERED SHELVES BLEND IN WITH THE BACKGROUND.

INTRODUCTION
PLANNING &
ASSESSMENT
TYPES OF
STORAGE
AREA BY AREA

Multipurpose areas

Multipurpose areas range from kitchen-diners to open-plan living spaces that serve various other functions, from cooking to eating. When you have different activities to reconcile within the same space, storage and spatial planning assume even more critical importance. If a living area is to remain a pleasant place to relax and entertain other people, storage should be as unobtrusive as possible, which means built-in arrangements are usually the best solution.

Try to arrange the basic layout so there is some degree of separation between different activities. Sociable and leisure activities can be grouped together; those that require more concentration need to be segregated in some way. An alcove, for example, can provide a sufficient enclosure for a small desk. Otherwise, the arrangement of furniture or spatial dividers, such as counters and half-height or half-width partitions, can serve to demarcate one zone from another. If your living room incorporates an eating area, placing a sofa so that its back faces towards the dining table can be explicit enough to mark the difference between the two areas. Rugs are also a good way of anchoring a seating arrangement and spelling out the difference between the part of the room devoted to relaxation and the remainder of the space.

ABOVE: SLIDING GLAZED PANELS CONCEAL A TV, DVDS AND BOARD GAMES. MEDIA EQUIPMENT CAN BE VERY DOMINANT IF IT IS OUT ON VIEW.

LEFT: A COMBINATION OF OPEN CUBBYHOLES AND CLOSED CUPBOARDS COMBINES STORAGE WITH DISPLAY. SOME FORM OF FITTED SOLUTION OFTEN WORKS BEST IN A MULTIPURPOSE SPACE.

continued

Multipurpose areas

Points to consider

- Decide whether it is possible to shift one of the functions that the area serves at present into a different location. Failing that, you might be able to find an alternative home for an entire category of possessions. Shelving a hallway would allow you to store books elsewhere and provide more breathing space.

- Multipurpose areas are often best treated as fitted rooms, with disparate activities concealed behind cupboard doors. Home offices can be remarkably compact and still remain efficient.

- In an open-plan living area, you can screen kitchen activity with a counter.

- Multifunctional furniture can help you save space. If the living area is the only place you can put up overnight guests, a good quality sofa bed is a sensible investment. You need to be prepared to spend money – cheap sofa beds are neither comfortable sofas nor comfortable beds. Alternatively, folding mattresses or upholstered foam blocks can do double duty as seating and spare beds.

- A built-in window seat can combine extra seating with a storage cache underneath for toys, games, CDs and DVDs.

- Pull-out or fold-down surfaces can be used for eating or as study areas. Any articulated element should be designed and constructed so that it can be smoothly operated.

ABOVE: A DESK SLOTTED INTO A MULTIPURPOSE SPACE PROVIDES A COMPACT AND DISCREET WORKING AREA.

RIGHT: A LONG HALF-HEIGHT PARTITION SERVES AS A HEADBOARD AND SCREENS A SLEEPING AREA FROM THE REST OF THE SPACE.

Living rooms

The living room is one of the most public areas in the home and the one in which the prime purpose must be relaxation, whatever other activities go on there. As the space where we tend to put our best foot forward, in a decorative sense, it is also often used as a place to display our favourite things.

The general aim should be to keep floors and other surfaces as clear as possible, which tends to mean using walls for shelving or other forms of open and concealed storage. Most living areas contain large pieces of furniture, such as sofas and armchairs, so it is usually best to go the fitted route rather than rely on freestanding pieces of storage furniture or multiple containers, which can be visually distracting.

Living rooms are, by their nature, shared spaces, which means that everyone in the household is likely to be using the space on a daily basis and perhaps in different ways. This, in turn, increases the likelihood of clutter building up. One good way of rethinking arrangements is to go into the living room and imagine that friends are coming over in half an hour. Which items would you tidy up? Which would you remove altogether? This type of assessment can give you a useful insight into ways in which living room storage can be better planned.

LEFT: WHATEVER YOU KEEP ON VIEW IN THE LIVING ROOM SHOULD MAKE SOME AESTHETIC CONTRIBUTION TO ITS OVERALL STYLE.

ABOVE: DEEP WOODEN SHELVES, PAINTED THE SAME COLOUR AS THE WOODWORK, READ AS PART OF THE EXISTING ARCHITECTURAL DETAIL.

continued

Living rooms

Options

- Shelving is the mainstay of living room storage and can house many of the belongings that are typically kept in there: books, magazines, CDs and DVDs. In a living room, shelving should blend in discreetly or be attractive enough to bear the scrutiny.
- A practical solution is to combine open book shelves with closed cupboards lower down for games, CDs and the like, which do not contribute much aesthetic interest.
- Living rooms have increasingly become places where TV and audio equipment are kept, as well as the disks that go along with them. While televisions are dominating features at the best of times, flat-screen TVs can loom exceptionally large. Concealing a TV behind a panel or within a cupboard can help maintain an air of relaxation when there is nothing worth watching.
- The pace of technological change means that many of us own the same film or album in different formats. Either dispose of the versions in the outdated formats or remove them to a different location.
- Keep favourite CDs and DVDs near where they will be played and store the rest in labelled containers to facilitate retrieval.
- Ensure that you have enough sockets for all your media equipment. Control cabling so that it does not snake dangerously across the floor.

ABOVE: THE FIREPLACE MAKES A BETTER FOCAL POINT FOR FURNITURE ARRANGEMENT THAN A TELEVISION SCREEN. A SMALL CUPBOARD AND A LOW TABLE TO EITHER SIDE PROVIDE PLACES TO KEEP BOOKS.

RIGHT: MEDIA EQUIPMENT, ALONG WITH CDS AND DVDS, IS UNOBTRUSIVELY SHELVED IN A CORNER.

Kitchens

Successful kitchens are all about good planning and systems of organization. When cooking is in full swing, you should be able to reach for ingredients and basic equipment without pause for thought. At the same time, you want to rest assured that provisions, fresh, frozen or preserved, are being stored in optimum conditions. From family nerve centre to eating area, kitchens increasingly serve additional roles which make their own storage demands.

Whether you opt for a fitted or unfitted arrangement, or a combination of the two, storage should be planned in the context of the 'working triangle' – the basic relationship between the refrigerator, sink and hob or stove. The distance between these three critical points should be no greater than 6m (20ft). Types of layout based on the working triangle include: single-line, L-shaped, U-shaped, galley, peninsula and island. Galley kitchens are ideal where space is limited. Island kitchens need more floor area.

The area between the sink and the stove is the most critical. Anything that you keep here should relate directly to preparing and cooking the food you eat on a regular basis. The rest of your provisions and equipment should be stored by type in cupboards or fitted units in the immediate vicinity.

LEFT: OPEN SHELVING MAKES A FEATURE OF A COLLECTION OF CROCKERY, THE TYPE OF CASUAL DISPLAY THAT BRINGS A KITCHEN TO LIFE.

ABOVE: THE LONGEST STRETCH OF WORKTOP SHOULD BE BETWEEN THE SINK AND THE COOKER OR HOB. FITTED CUPBOARDS KEEP EQUIPMENT NEATLY STOWED.

continued

Kitchens

Points to consider

- It is a good idea to periodically review your kitchen provisions and equipment. Discard food that is past its use-by date. Cast a critical eye over utensils, equipment and small appliances. Any item you hardly ever use is ripe for disposal.

- If you find yourself throwing out a lot of fresh food, it is time to review your shopping habits. Do not be tempted to buy in bulk simply for the sake of a special offer.

- Dried herbs and spices are best kept out of direct light in a cool, dark cupboard, preferably in a rack for easy retrieval.

- Accessories such as drawer dividers, trays and adjustable shelves allow you to customize the interior of fitted units to make full use of the available storage space.

- What you keep out on view – on open shelves, hanging from a rack or rail, on the worktop – should be in daily use. Small appliances that you do not use very often should be stored away from the worktop.

- Store knives in knife blocks, on a magnetic strip or in a shallow drawer by themselves.

- Make sure that your refrigerator is operating efficiently. Do not position it near a heat source, defrost it regularly and do not overstock it. Practise good food hygiene: keep raw food separate from cooked food.

- Freezers work best when they are fully stocked. Label and date home-frozen and preserved food.

ABOVE: WINE THAT IS GOING TO BE KEPT FOR A PERIOD OF TIME REQUIRES SPECIFIC CONDITIONS. THIS UNIT ALLOWS BOTTLES TO BE STORED FLAT.

RIGHT: ITEMS SUCH AS TEAS, COFFEE AND SUGAR CAN BE KEPT NEAR THE KETTLE IN AIRTIGHT CONTAINERS.

Eating areas

Separate dining areas are becoming more of a rarity these days, with many people opting to include an eating area in the kitchen or as part of an open-plan living/eating/cooking space. Whichever arrangement you choose, you will need dedicated storage space near the table for crockery, cutlery and glassware. Ideally, this should not be too far away from the kitchen sink or dishwasher.

Dressers or retro-style maid-savers can provide enough storage space for everyday glasses, dishes and cutlery. Alternatively, you can use fitted units or open racks or shelves. Bear in mind that whatever you keep out on display should be in regular use to prevent dust and grease from building up.

- Shallow shelves are ideal for storing crockery and glassware. Items do not get pushed to the back and there is less chance of chipping.
- Sort crockery into like with like (size, pattern and type) and keep piles no greater than six to eight items.
- Plate racks keep plates from scraping against each other.
- Drawer dividers are essential for organizing cutlery. Silver flatware needs to be kept separate from stainless steel, either in felt-lined canteens or felt bags.
- Group glassware by size and type. Do not store glasses upside down on their rims.
- Delicate cups should not be hung from their handles, which is their weakest point.

LEFT: A RUG CAN BE AN EFFECTIVE WAY OF DEFINING AN EATING AREA WITHIN A MULTIPURPOSE SPACE. THIS ONE MIRRORS THE CIRCULAR TABLE.

ABOVE: THE TRADITIONAL KITCHEN DRESSER REMAINS AN EVER-POPULAR STORAGE SOLUTION FOR EVERYDAY CROCKERY AND TABLEWARE.

Bathrooms

Bathrooms, like kitchens, feature fixed points of servicing. Together with the fact that they tend to be relatively small spaces, this means that fitted storage is often the best bet. Built-in storage allows you to integrate the sink, toilet, bathtub and shower to create a neat, unified effect. Many bathroom specialists, as well as large retailers, provide an in-house design service to help you make the most of the space available, or you could commission a designer, builder or carpenter for a bespoke result.

Options

- Washstands come in various shapes and sizes, from wall-hung cabinets and tall shallow cupboards to floor units with inset sinks.
- If you opt for wall-hung toilet pans and sinks, you can conceal the cistern, soil pipe and plumbing runs behind a dummy wall that also incorporates storage space.
- Enclosing the bathtub in a panelled framework provides additional shelving space at the head and the foot. It may also be possible to incorporate cupboards behind the panelling.
- Freestanding storage furniture, such as armoires and chests, are really only suitable for large bathrooms.
- Wet rooms, where the shower drains directly into the floor, tend to rule out much in the way of bathroom storage, since anything you keep there is likely to become damp.

ABOVE: A SINK AND WASHSTAND IS NEATLY SLOTTED INTO A RECESS. THE WOODEN SURROUND PROVIDES A CONVENIENT PLACE FOR SOAP AND TOOTHBRUSHES.

RIGHT: A FREESTANDING ARMOIRE MAKES A HANDSOME LINEN STORE IN A SPACIOUS BATHROOM. THE BACK-TO-THE-WALL TOILET HAS A CISTERN CONCEALED BEHIND A DUMMY PANEL.

continued

Bathrooms

Points to consider

- Most cosmetics have a shelf-life of six months or so. Old medicines may be harmful. It is worth going through your bathroom cabinets and removing cosmetics, medicines and remedies that are past their use-by date.
- In a shared bathroom, it is useful to provide dedicated storage for each member of the family. A pegboard mounted on the wall or on the back of the bathroom door can be used to suspend individual cosmetics bags.
- Keep bulk supplies of toilet paper out of the bathroom. Similarly, most bathrooms are too small to house your entire stock of bath linen.
- Bathroom products and accessories that you use every day can be kept on open shelves.

- It is much more pleasant to conceal cleaning products from view or store them elsewhere.
- Wall cabinets that combine storage space with a mirrored front and integral lighting make good use of available space.
- Toothbrushes should be suspended in a wall-mounted toothbrush holder or similar so that they can drain after use.
- Soap should be kept on a wire rack or on a perforated or ridged dish.
- Heated towel rails keep towels warm and dry, as well as supplying background heat.
- Small trolleys make an attractive way of organizing spare towels and bath products.
- Hampers and baskets make good improvised containers for bathroom storage.

LEFT: A LOW WOODEN BENCH PROVIDES A STREAMLINED UNOBTRUSIVE STORAGE PLACE FOR FRESH TOWELS AND OTHER BATHROOM ACCESSORIES.

ABOVE: FITTED LAYOUTS ALLOW YOU TO INTEGRATE FIXTURES, CONCEAL PLUMBING AND BUILD-IN STORAGE SPACE TO CREATE A HARMONIOUS WHOLE.

Bedrooms

We look to our bedrooms to provide private, comfortable surroundings where we can wind down at the end of the day and wake up refreshed the next morning. In most cases, the bedroom is also where we store the bulk of our wardrobe. Careful planning is necessary to ensure that this essential storage function does not undermine the bedroom's prime role as personal refuge.

The bedroom is necessarily dominated by a large piece of furniture and for this reason it is generally better to install fitted clothes storage rather than encroach upon the floor area with other freestanding pieces of storage furniture. However, if your bedroom includes alcoves or recesses, chests of drawers can be sited there, keeping the main floor space free.

An essential first step is to carry out a thorough review of what you own. Studies have shown that most people only wear 20 per cent of their wardrobe, which means that most of the storage space devoted to clothing is wasted. Get rid of anything you have not worn for a year or more, as well as clothing that does not fit, does not suit you or needs expensive repair. Rotating clothing on a seasonal basis can also help ease the pressure on space.

ABOVE: THE BULK OF A TRADITIONAL WARDROBE IS MINIMIZED BY ITS WHITE PAINTED FINISH. STORAGE CONTAINERS FIT NEATLY IN THE AREA UNDER THE BED.

RIGHT: SHELVED ALCOVES DOUBLE UP AS BEDSIDE TABLES AND A PLACE TO KEEP BOOKS.

continued

Bedrooms

Points to consider

- As well as reviewing your clothing, take a long hard look at whatever else you are keeping in your bedroom and clear away any possessions that do not belong there. Some people keep a library under their beds; others build up a collection of magazines or DVDs.

- To store your clothes you will need a combination of hanging space, double-hung if possible, and drawers or shelves for items that are best stored flat.

- Only keep a limited number of items out on view. Open shelves and rails expose clothing to dust and fading from sunlight.

- Shoes can be racked on rails at the bottom of your closet, stored in cubbyholes, fabric bags or lidded containers.

- Make use of the space under the bed to store bulky items, such as spare blankets and jumpers. Some beds have integral storage drawers or compartments.

- Do not overfill clothes storage. Moths thrive where clothes are tightly packed.

- Customize the interiors of cupboards and drawers with dividers, racks and rails for storing small items and accessories.

- It is useful to organize your wardrobe so that clothes of a similar type, length and colour are grouped together.

- Evening wear and formal suits need extra protection and should be kept in cotton garment bags.

ABOVE: A FITTED BEDSIDE TABLE WITH A DRAWER DOES NOT ENCROACH UPON FLOOR AREA. THE WALL-MOUNTED LIGHT CAN BE ANGLED FOR COMFORTABLE READING.

LEFT: FITTED CLOTHES STORAGE IS LESS DOMINANT IN A BEDROOM. THE TASK LIGHTS POSITIONED OVER THE CLOSETS ARE A USEFUL FEATURE.

Dressing rooms

While a separate dressing room sounds like the height of luxury, it can represent a very effective use of space. Equally, removing clothing from the bedroom altogether makes it a more peaceful and contemplative place.

A dressing room does not have to be large to be worthwhile. A walk-in closet or narrow hallway lined with fitted closets and shelves on both sides will generally provide enough room for most of your clothing. It is important to site the area either near the bedroom or the bathroom, where clothes are most often taken off and put on. Another option is to co-opt a small spare bedroom as a dressing area.

■ Storage specialists produce closet systems for dressing areas (or fitted storage within the bedroom itself).
■ You can commission bespoke designs from a skilled carpenter.
■ Simple dressing rooms can be equipped with a mixture of rails, drawers and shelves concealed behind doors or sliding panels.
■ A full-length mirror is indispensable.
■ Good lighting is important. You will need a combination of good background lighting and information light within cupboards or closets.

ABOVE: A COMPACT DRESSING AREA COMPRISES A HANGING RAIL AND A SIMPLE MODULAR UNIT FOR CLOTHES AND OTHER ACCESSORIES.

RIGHT: A BESPOKE DRESSING ROOM CONTAINS EVERY TYPE OF CLOTHES STORAGE FROM DOUBLE HANGING CLOSETS TO DRAWERS, SHELVING AND CUBBYHOLES.

Children's rooms

Children grow fast and accumulate possessions at an alarming rate. Flexible, accessible storage systems are essential. Miniaturized items of storage furniture rarely earn their keep. Instead, think about solutions that can be adapted to each development stage. These include bookcases, built-in shelving, chests of drawers, hanging storage and containers.

Ages & stages

- Keep pace with the rate of change by setting aside regular times for review when you can discard outgrown clothing, toys and games. Items in good condition can be handed down to younger family members or friends, or donated to charity.
- Baby and toddler equipment, such as buggies and high chairs, can be bulky. Collapsible designs are more space-saving.
- Small children need plenty of floor space to play. Consider room allocation: a large room that doubles up as a playroom and bedroom can ease the pressure on the rest of the home. You can review arrangements later when children require separate rooms.
- For children of school age and over, modular systems that combine storage with beds can be a good idea.
- Low rails and pegs for clothing and kit bags are more accessible for small children.
- Provide plenty of display space for toys, books artwork and other mementoes. Children like to be surrounded by their favourite things.

ABOVE: A WALL-HUNG CUPBOARD KEEPS BOOKS HANDY AND DOUBLES UP AS A PLACE TO DISPLAY TOYS.

LEFT: MODULAR BOXES MAKE GREAT STOWING PLACES FOR ALL KINDS OF CHILDREN'S BELONGINGS.

continued

Children's rooms

Containers

From coloured plastic boxes to storage jars, containers of various kinds are indispensable for children's storage. In the early months, most of your child's toys will probably fit into a single container – choose one that is sturdy but also easily portable. As your child acquires more possessions, sort toys by type. Games or toys with multiple parts can be organized into colour-coded boxes. Containers on castors that can be wheeled under the bed are also useful, as are modular and stackable designs.

Daily routines

- Keep important documents, such as birth certificates, immunization records and school reports in a dedicated file.
- Routine administration, such as school notices and schedules, should be kept together in one place, with the other household paperwork.
- A calendar put up in a prominent position can be a useful reminder of key dates.

Safety

- Ensure that all tall and heavy items of storage furniture are bracketed securely against the wall to prevent them from toppling or being pulled over.
- High-level or bunk beds must conform to safety standards. Children younger than five or six should never sleep in an upper bunk.
- Avoid glass doors or unit fronts at low level.
- Store all toxic substances under lock and key, including cleaners, paints, glues, garden products and medicines.

ABOVE: ACCESSIBLE STORAGE HELPS TO ENCOURAGE CHILDREN TO TAKE CARE OF THEIR THINGS.

RIGHT: A BABY'S CHANGING TRAY THAT FITS OVER THE COT IS A GREAT SPACE SAVER IN THIS SMALL BEDROOM.

Working areas

Laundry and utility rooms, workshops and home offices all require good systems of organization if they are to serve their various purposes efficiently. These functional spaces, however, tend to be out of public view and are often used as dumping grounds, becoming silted up with objects and equipment that have little to do with the designated activity. Begin with a good clear-out and then arrange tools, equipment and supplies in a logical fashion that makes tasks easier to carry out.

Laundry & utility rooms

- A separate utility room is a good place to keep other household cleaning equipment, such as vacuum cleaners, mops and buckets. Do not store garden tools in the same place.
- If you do not have space for a utility room, you can site laundry machines in a bathroom or incorporate them into a fitted kitchen. Alternatively, a washing machine can be housed in a closet with shelving above for linen storage. Pull-out or fold-down ironing boards are also good space-saving devices.
- Linen should be stored in a location that is warm, dry and accessible to bedrooms and bathrooms, such as an airing cupboard, separate closet, chest or chest of drawers.
- It is a good idea to rotate sheets and towels so that they receive equal wear.

ABOVE: SHELVES BUILT INTO AN ALCOVE HOUSE SPARE BATH LINEN AND LAUNDRY EQUIPMENT. GOOD ORGANIZATION MAKES ROUTINE CHORES EASIER AND MORE PLEASANT TO ACCOMPLISH.

LEFT: A SEPARATE HOME OFFICE, WELL AWAY FROM THE REST OF THE HOUSEHOLD, IS ESSENTIAL IF YOU ARE GOING TO BE WORKING FROM HOME FULL TIME.

continued

Working areas

Home office

- Choose a location that offers psychological and physical separation from the main run of the household: a converted attic, a spare room, a generous landing or an outbuilding such as a shed.
- Keep items used everyday close at hand, on or near the worktop or desk.
- Supplies and files relating to current projects need to be stored in an accessible location on shelves, in drawers or in filing cabinets.
- Archives relating to your career history, including financial records and tax returns can be kept in deep storage.
- Modular containers, such as box files, bring a pleasing element of visual coherence to open storage systems.

Workshops, garages & sheds

- Many people accumulate tools and rarely use them. Rather than storing them, consider borrowing or hiring tools on the infrequent occasions when you need to use them.
- Separate tools into type. Keep garden tools, for example, separate from those used for car maintenance.
- Hanging and racking systems allow you to exploit wall space.
- Many companies produce robust storage systems, such as shelving units, specifically designed for garage or workshop use.
- Toolboxes with interior compartments and tiered trays are good for organizing small tools. Keep nails and screws of different sizes and types in separate labelled containers.

LEFT: WICKER BASKETS AND SIMPLE CONTAINERS OF VARIOUS KINDS ORGANIZE TOOLS, MATERIALS AND SUPPLIES IN A HOME STUDIO.

RIGHT: A LANDING OR THE CORNER OF A MEZZANINE CAN PROVIDE ENOUGH SPACE FOR A SIMPLE WORKTOP.

Index

Acknowledgements

The publisher would like to thank Red Cover Picture Library for their kind permission to reproduce the following photographs:

2 David George; 6–7 Chris Tubbs (Designer: Maiden); 10 Catherine Gratwicke; 11 Winfried Heinze; 12 Simon Scarboro; 13 Paul Ryan-Goff; 16 Mike Daines; 17 Andrew Wood; 18 Alun Callender; 19 Winfried Heinze (Designer: Lisa Weeks, Furniture Designer: Amy Somerville); 20 Alun Callender; 21 Winfried Heinze (Designer: Orla Kiely); 22 Ed Reeve (Designer: Jona Warbey); 23 Richard Powers; 24 Paul Massey; 25 Sarah Hogan (Stylist: Katie Sellers); 26 Practical Pictures; 27 Johnny Bouchier; 28 Simon Scarboro; 29 Karyn Millet (Designers: Michael Fullen/Susan Adams); 30 Ashley Morrison; 31 James Balston (Architect: David Cook & Akoko Kubayashi); 32 Douglas Gibb; 33 David George; 36 Jake Fitzjones; 37 Paul Massey; 38 James Balston (Designer: Sally Dernie); 39 Fabio Lombrici; 40 Henry Wilson; 41 Simon McBride; 42 Andrew Twort (Designer: Michael Reeves); 43 Lucinda Symons; 44 Henry Wilson; 45 Chris Tubbs; 46 Simon McBride; 47 Winfried Heinze (Designer: Orla Kiely); 48 Sophie Munro; 49 Paul Massey; 50 Simon Scarboro; 51 Andrew Wood; 52 Alun Callender; 53 Paul Ryan-Goff; 54 David George; 55 Henry Wilson; 56 James Balston (Architect: Gianni Botsford); 57 Simon Scarboro; 58 Jake Fitzjones; 59 Jake Fitzjones (Mowlem & Co); 60 Chris Tubbs (Designer: Maiden); 61 Grant Scott; 62 Winfried Heinze; 63 Graham Atkins-Hughes; 64 Winfried Heinze; 65 Debi Treloar; 66 Victoria Gomez; 67 Jo Tyler (Architect: Angus Shepard-Powell Tuck); 68 Kim Sayer; 69 Chris Tubbs (Architect: Honky, Designer: Honky Design); 70 Michael Freeman; 71 Alun Callender; 72 Chris Tubbs; 73 Winfried Heinze (Designer: Orla Kiely); 74 Troy Campbell (Designer: Briggs Solomon); 78 Mark York; 79 Christopher Drake (Designer: Annie Stevens); 80 Winfried Heinze; 81 Henry Wilson; 82 Steve Dalton; 83 Graham Atkins-Hughes; 84 Paul Massey; 85 Paul Ryan-Goff; 86 Holly Joliffe; 87 Mark York (Designer: Gul Coskun); 88 Simon McBride; 89 Nick Carter; 90 David Prince; 91 Ed Reeve; 92 Paul Ryan-Goff; 93 Jake Fitzjones (Designer: Shani Zion); 94 Warren Smith; 95 Ed Reeve (Designer: Monica Mauti Equihua); 96 Debi Treloar; 97 Grant Govier; 98 Jake Fitzjones; 99 Ken Hayden; 100 Jake Fitzjones; 101 Winfried Heinze (Designer: Emily Todhunter); 102 Redcover; 103 James Balston; 104 Dan Duchars; 105 Jake Fitzjones (Architect: Stuart Forbes Associates, Company: The London Basement Company); 106 Henry Wilson (Designer: Maria Speake); 107 Paul Massey; 108 Tria Giovan; 109 Ken Hayden.

Except for the following photograph:
page 75 Chris Tubbs/Conran Octopus.

First published in 2010 by Conran Octopus Ltd,
a part of Octopus Publishing Group,
Endeavour House,
189 Shaftesbury Avenue,
London WC2H 8JG
www.octopusbooks.co.uk

A Hachette UK Company
www.hachette.co.uk

Distributed in the United States and Canada by Octopus Books USA, c/o Hachette Book Group USA, 237 Park Avenue, New York, NY 10017 USA

Text copyright © Conran Octopus Ltd 2010
Design and layout copyright © Conran Octopus Ltd 2010

British Library Cataloguing-in-Publication Data.
A catalogue record for this book is available from the British Library.

Consultant Editor: Elizabeth Wilhide

Publisher: Lorraine Dickey
Managing Editor: Sybella Marlow
Editor: Bridget Hopkinson

Art Director: Jonathan Christie
Picture Researcher: Liz Boyd
Design Assistant: Mayumi Hashimoto

Production: Caroline Alberti

ISBN: 978 1 84091 550 1
Printed in China